THE ART OF THE

KAMA SUTRA

Douglas Mannering

A Compilation of Works from the
BRIDGEMAN ART LIBRARY

‖ •PARRAGON• ‖

Kama Sutra

This edition first published in Great Britain in 1994
by Parragon Book Service Limited

© 1994 Parragon Book Service Limited

ISBN 1 85813 651 2

Printed in Italy

Editor: Alexa Stace
Designer: Robert Mathias

The publishers would like to thank Joanna Hartley
at the Bridgeman Art Library for her invaluable help

Kama Sutra

The *Kama Sutra* (Aphorisms on Love) was written in India some time between the 1st and 5th centuries AD. Its author is said to have been Mallanga Vatsyayana, but almost nothing is known of him for certain, beyond the text of the *Kama Sutra* itself, which states that it 'was compiled, according to the precepts of the Scriptures, for the benefit of the world, by Vatsyayana while he was leading the life of a religious student and wholly engaged in the contemplation of the Divine'.

The Scriptures in question were, of course, the sacred books of Hinduism, the dominant religion of India, and this explains how a handbook on profane love could be compiled by a religious student. Unlike most major religions, Hinduism is not exclusively other-worldly in outlook, but views human activity as directed towards three ends: Dharma, the acquisition of religious merit; Artha, the achievement of social and political goals, including personal wealth; and Kama, which comprises love and the other pleasures of the senses. In Vatsyayana's day, although religious merit was certainly regarded as important, Artha and Kama were not only held to be legitimate but, properly pursued, had their own share in the divine scheme of things. In Kama, for example, and specifically in sexual union, a man and a woman re-enacted the very creation of the cosmos.

Dharma, Artha and Kama all became the subjects of

classic texts which were intended to be widely read. The *Kama Sutra* claims that it is essentially an abridgement of much earlier works but, if so, its quality was such that these texts have vanished without trace. In India the *Kama Sutra* became the definitive guide to human relations – so much so that Hindu literature is full of direct references to it, while its influence on sculpture and painting is unmistakable.

In the West, the reputation of the *Kama Sutra* rests largely on its candid descriptions of varieties of the sex act; and the illlustrations in this book demonstrate that this aspect of it has also been influential in its native land. But passages directly descriptive of sex actually take up quite a small proportion of the book, which also treats such topics as the appropriate lifestyle for a man about town, courtship and marriage, the duties of a wife, techniques of seduction, the role of courtesans, and ways of enhancing one's personal attractiveness ranging from magical incantations to recipes for enlarging the lingam, or male sex organ.

One of the most notable features of the *Kama Sutra* is its objective, unprejudiced tone: Vatsyayana describes what men and women are and do, only occasionally reminding the reader that a description is not necessarily a recommendation, and that some practices may be dubious in religious law or best avoided if they run counter to local custom. By and large he is remarkably tolerant, frequently putting it forward as his view that lovers should do whatever suits them best.

This was strikingly different from the puritan tradition in the West which reached its culmination in the Victorian era. Moreover the *Kama Sutra*, as well as being explicit, based itself on propositions that were repugnant to most Victorians – for example, that women could experience sexual pleasure, and that consequently skill and consideration were required of men.

The importance of these truths, as well as their genuine interest in Indian literature, influenced the Victorian translators of the *Kama Sutra,* F. F. Arbuthnot and Sir Richard Burton. Even publishing the book in English for private circulation, as they did in 1883, was an act of some daring; the first edition intended for the general public only appeared in 1963, after landmark legal decisions had made a prosecution unlikely.

In India the handbook written in aphorisms or sutras – brief, pithy, unadorned statements – is a traditional literary form, and one which lends itself to extensive quotation. The extracts in this anthology are intended to give the reader an idea of the book's real scope. For all its 'modern' tolerance in sexual matters, the world of the *Kama Sutra* is also a product of its time, and of an ancient caste society in which the harem was jealously (if often unavailingly) guarded, the sexual 'double standard' operated, body markings might be lucky or unlucky, and knowledge of magic and sorcery belonged among the 64 arts. Some of all this will be found in the extracts, but the abiding impression, reinforced by a selection of Indian miniatures which reflect the ethos of the *Kama Sutra,* is of a highly civilized society which took its pleasures seriously, ceremoniously and gracefully.

The text is based on Arbuthnot and Burton's translation, edited with the modern reader in mind.

What is Kama?

IN THE BEGINNING, the Lord of All Beings created men and women, and in the form of commandments in one hundred thousand chapters laid down rules for regulating their existence with regard to Dharma, Artha and Kama: that is, the acquisition of religious merit, wealth, and love and pleasure. Kama is the enjoyment of appropriate objects by the five senses of hearing, feeling, seeing, tasting and smelling, assisted by the mind and the soul. Its essential feature lies in the contact between the organ of sense and its object; and the consciousness of pleasure which arises from that contact is called Kama. Kama is to be learned from the *Kama Sutra*, which means 'Aphorisms on Love', and from the way people behave in the world.

Why Kama Should Be Studied

SOME LEARNED MEN say that Kama, being a thing which is practised even by the brute creation, and which is found everywhere, does not require study or need to have a work written about it. But this is not so. Sexual intercourse, being a thing dependent on man and woman, requires the application of proper means by them; and those means are to be learned from the Kama Shastra, or science of love. The inapplicability of proper means, which we see in the brute creation, is caused by their congress being unrestrained, by the fact that the females among them are only fit for sexual intercourse at certain seasons and no more, and because their intercourse is not preceded by thought of any kind.

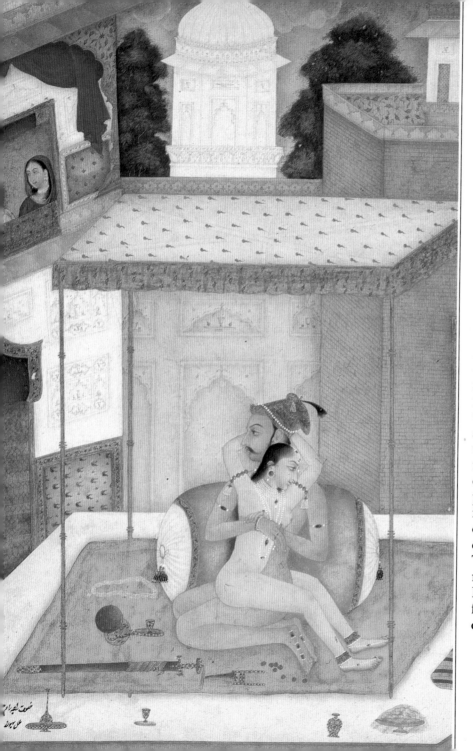

Of Love and Wealth

THOSE WHO ARE INCLINED to believe that Artha, wealth, is the chief object of life, argue thus. Pleasures should not be sought for, because they are obstacles to the acquisition of Dharma (religious merit) and Artha, which are both superior to them. Pleasures also bring a man into distress, and into contact with low persons; they cause him to commit unrighteous deeds, and produce impurity in him; they make him heedless of the future, and encourage carelessness and levity. It is notorious, moreover, that many men who have given themselves up to pleasure alone have ruined themselves, their families and their relations. But this objection cannot be sustained, for pleasures, being as necessary for the existence and wellbeing of the body as food, are consequently equally required. They are, moreover, the results of Dharma and Artha. Pleasures are, therefore, to be followed with moderation and caution.

Of Women and the Kama Sutra

PEOPLE SHOULD STUDY the *Kama Sutra* and the arts and sciences associated with it, as well as the arts and sciences involved in Dharma and Artha. Even young maids should study the *Kama Sutra*, along with its arts and sciences, before marriage, and after it they should continue to do so with the consent of their husbands. Here some learned men object, arguing that females, who are not allowed to study any of the sciences, ought not to study the *Kama Sutra* either. But Vatsyayana is of the opinion that this objection does not hold good, for women already know the practice of *Kama Sutra*, and that practice is itself derived from the Kama Shastra, or the science of Kama. Some women, such as daughters of princes and their ministers, and public women, are actually versed in the Kama Shastra.

The 64 Arts

THE FOLLOWING are some of the 64 arts to be studied by a woman, together with the *Kama Sutra*. Dancing, singing and playing musical instruments. Writing and drawing. Tattooing. Adorning an idol with rice and flowers. Spreading and arranging beds or couches of flowers. Colouring the teeth, garments, hair, nails and body. Fixing stained glass into a floor. Making beds and arranging carpets and cushions. Playing musical glasses filled with water. Picture making, stringing garlands, and preparing perfumes. Magic or sorcery. Cooking and sewing. Verse-making games. The art of acquiring property belonging to someone else by means of incantations. Knowledge of architecture, gardening, languages, disguises, gambling, gymnastics and the art of war.

Uses of the 64 Arts

THE DAUGHTER of a king or the daughter of a minister, being learned in the 64 arts, can make her husband look with favour on her, even though he may have thousands of other wives. And in the same manner, if a wife becomes separated from her husband, and falls into distress, she can support herself easily, even in a foreign country, through her mastery of these arts. Merely knowing them gives attractiveness to a woman, though putting them into practice may or may not be possible, depending on circumstances. A man who is versed in these arts, who is eloquent and acquainted with the arts of gallantry, very soon gains the hearts of women, even when he has been acquainted with them for only a short time.

Where to Receive a Woman

THE OUTER ROOM, balmy with rich perfumes, should contain a canopied bed which is soft and agreeable to the sight, covered with a clean white cloth, low in the middle, with garlands and bunches of flowers upon it and two pillows, one at the top, another at the bottom. There should also be a sort of couch, and at its head a stool, on which should be placed fragrant unguents for the night, as well as flowers, pots containing collyrium and other sweet-smelling substances, things used for perfuming the mouth, and the bark of the common citron tree. Near the couch, on the ground, there should be a pot for spitting, a box containing ornaments, and also a lute hanging from a peg made of the tooth of an elephant, a board for drawing, a pot containing perfume, some books, and some garlands of yellow amaranth flowers.

Social Diversions

FESTIVALS, social gatherings, drinking parties and picnics. Spending nights playing with dice. Going out on moonlit nights. Keeping the festive day in honour of spring. Plucking the sprouts and fruits of the mango trees. Eating the fibres of lotuses. Eating the tender ears of corn. Picnicking in the forests when the trees have their new foliage. The Udakakashvedika, or sporting in water. Decorating each other with the flowers of some trees. Pelting each other with the flowers of the kadamba tree, and many other sports which may be either known to the whole country or local specialities. These and similar amusements can be followed by a person who diverts himself in company with a courtesan, and also by a courtesan who can do the same in company with her maidservants or with men of her acquaintance.

Of Confidantes and Go-betweens

A MESSENGER, sent between lovers, should possess the following qualities. Skilfulness. Boldness. Ability to interpret men's intentions from outward signs. Absence of shyness. Good manners. Knowledge of the appropriate times and places for performing various actions. Ingenuity in business. Quick comprehension. And swiftness in resource. A female astrologer, a female servant, a female beggar, or a female artist are well acquainted with the business of the go-between, and very soon gain the confidence of other women. One of them can make any two persons become enemies, or extol the loveliness of any woman with great effect, or praise her sexual arts. Go-betweens can also speak highly of the love of a man, of his sexual skills, and of the desire for him felt by other women. A go-between can, by her artful talk, unite a woman with a man even though he may not have been thought of by her, and can also bring back to a woman a lover who has left her.

Detail

Kinds of Sexual Union

ACCORDING TO THE SIZE of his lingam, or sexual organ, men are divided into three classes, namely hare men, bull men and horse men. Likewise a woman, according to the depth of her yoni, is either a female deer, a mare, or a female elephant. There are consequently three equal unions between persons of corresponding dimensions, and there are six unequal unions, when the dimensions do not correspond, making nine in all. There are also nine kinds of union according to the force of passion or carnal desire felt by each of the partners. And lastly, according to the time that elapses between arousal and satisfaction, there are three kinds of men and women, the short-timed, the moderate-timed, and the long-timed; so that of these, once more, there are nine kinds of union.

Varieties of Sexual Union

SINCE THERE ARE nine kinds of sexual union with regard to dimensions, force of passion and time, respectively, the various combinations of them would result in innumerable kinds of union. Therefore in each particular kind of sexual union, men should use such means as they may think suitable in the circumstances. On the first occasion of sexual union the passion of the male is intense and his time is short, but in subsequent unions on the same day, the reverse of this is the case. With the female, however, the opposite is true, for at the first time her passion is weak, and consequently her time is long, but on subsequent occasions on the same day her passion is intense and her time short, until her passion is satisfied.

On the Different Kinds of Love

MEN LEARNED in the humanities are of the opinion that love is of four kinds. Love resulting from the constant and continual performance of some act, as for instance the love of sexual intercourse, the love of hunting, the love of drinking and the love of gambling. Love which is felt for things to which we are not habituated, and which proceeds entirely from ideas: that is, love resulting from imagination. The love which is mutual on both sides and proved to be true, when each looks upon the other as his or her very own. And finally the love resulting from the perception of external objects; the pleasure which it affords is superior to the pleasure of the other kinds of love.

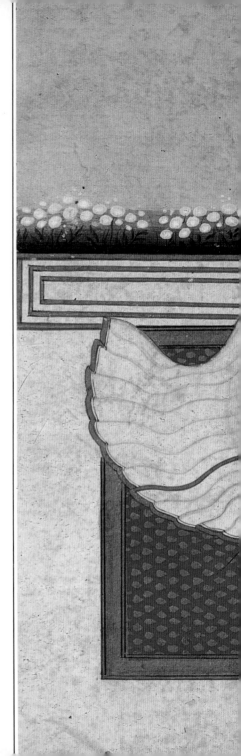

इंद्रासननामः॥दृहा॥कुंजरवरचक्रंबरी:तरुणी रूपनिधं
नःकांमीकोमनकांममें:सममेंचतुर्भुजांनः॥१९॥

Embraces

WHEN A WOMAN, clinging to a man as a creeper twines round a tree, bends his head down to hers with the desire of kissing him, softly makes the sound of sut sut, embraces him and looks lovingly towards him, this is known as Jataveshtitaka, an embrace like the twining of a creeper. And when a woman, having placed one of her feet on the foot of her lover and the other foot on one of his thighs, passes one of her arms round his back and the other on his shoulders, softly makes the sounds of singing and cooing, and wishes, as it were, to climb up him in order to enjoy a kiss, this is known as Vrikshadhirudhaka, an embrace like climbing a tree.

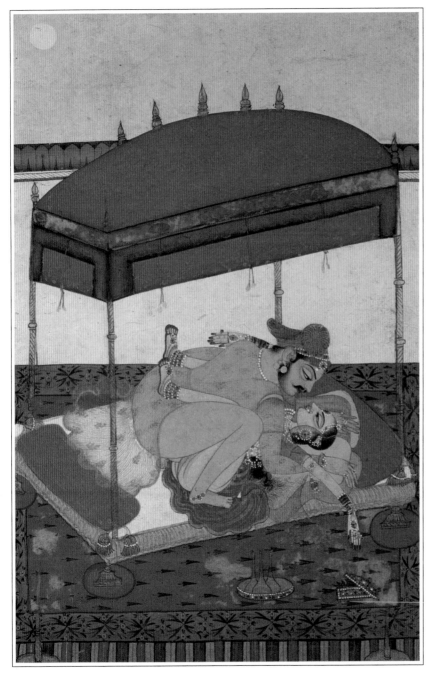

Sexual Embraces

WHEN LOVERS LIE on a bed, and embrace each other so closely that the arms and thighs of the one are encircled by the arms and thighs of the other, and are, as it were, rubbing up against them, this is known as Tila-Tandulaka, an embrace like the mixture of sesamum seed with rice. And when a man and a woman are very much in love with each other and, not thinking of any pain or hurt, embrace each other as if they were entering into each other's bodies, while the woman is either sitting on the lap of the man, or in front of him, or on a bed, this is known as Kshiraniraka, an embrace like a mixture of milk and water. These two kinds of embrace take place at the time of sexual union.

More on the Subject of Embraces

SUVARNANABHA lists four ways of embracing simple members of the body: the embrace of the thighs; the embrace of the jaghana, or the part of the body between the navel and the thighs; the embrace of the breasts; and the embrace of the forehead. The whole subject of embracing is of such a nature that men who ask questions about it, or who hear about it, or who talk about it, acquire thereby a desire for enjoyment. Even those embraces that are not mentioned in the Kama Shastra should be practised at the time of sexual enjoyment if they are in any way conducive to the increase of love or passion. The rules of the Shastra apply so long as the passion of man is middling, but when the wheel of love is once set in motion, there is then no Shastra and no order.

On Kissing

IT IS SAID by some that there is no fixed time or order between the embrace, the kiss, and pressing or scratching with the nails or fingers, but that all these things should generally be done before sexual union takes place, while striking and making various sounds generally takes place at the time of the union. Vatsyayana, however, thinks that anything may be done at any time, for love does not care for time or order. On the occasion of the first congress, kissing and the other things under discussion should be engaged in moderately, should not be continued for a long time, and should be done alternately. On subsequent occasions, however, the situation is reversed and moderation will not be necessary: all of these things may continue for a long time and, for the purpose of kindling love, they may be all done at the same time.

Kinds of Kissing

WHEN A WOMAN looks at the face of her lover while he is asleep and kisses it to show her desire. When a woman kisses her lover while he is engaged in business, or quarrelling with her, or otherwise distracted. When a lover coming home late at night kisses his beloved, who is asleep on her bed, in order to show her his desire. When a person kisses the reflection of the person he loves in a mirror, in water, or on a wall. When, in the presence of his beloved, a person kisses a child sitting on his lap, or a picture, or an image or figure. And when at night, in a crowded place, a man coming up to a woman kisses a finger of her hand if she is standing, or a toe of her foot if she is sitting, or when a woman who is massaging her lover's body places her face on his thigh (as if she feels sleepy) so as to inflame his passion, and kisses his thigh or great toe.

On Pressing, Scratching and Biting

WHEN LOVE BECOMES intense, pressing with the nails or scratching the body with them is practised, and it is done on the following occasions: on the first visit; at the time of setting out on a journey; on the return from a journey; at the time when an angry lover has been conciliated; and lastly when the woman is intoxicated. But pressing with the nails is not a usual thing except with those who are intensely passionate; it is employed, together with biting, by those to whom the practice is agreeable. All the places that can be kissed are also the places that can be bitten, except the upper lip, the interior of the mouth, and the eyes. But Suvarnanabha is of the opinion that when the impetuosity of passion is excessive, the places need not be considered.

On Striking

SEXUAL INTERCOURSE can be compared to a quarrel, on account of the contrarities of love and its tendency to flare up into disputes. The place of striking with passion is the body, and on the body the special places are: the shoulders; the head; the space between the breasts; the back; the jaghana or middle part of the body; and the sides. Such passionate actions and amorous gesticulations or movements, which arise on the spur of the moment, are as irregular as dreams. A horse having once attained the fifth degree of motion goes on with blind speed, regardless of pits, ditches and posts in his way; and in the same manner a loving pair become blind with passion in the heat of congress, and go on with great impetuosity, paying not the least regard to excess.

Congress with a Deer Woman

THE DEER WOMAN, who possesses the smallest yoni, should adopt one of the following three ways of lying down: the widely opened position; the yawning position; and the position of the wife of Indra. When she lowers her head and raises her middle parts, it is called the widely opened position. At such a time the man should apply some unguent, so as to make the entrance easy. When she raises her thighs and keeps them wide apart and engages in congress, it is called the yawning position. And when she places her thighs with her legs doubled on them upon her sides, and thus engages in congress, it is called the position of Indrani, which is learned only by practice.

Clasping and Twining Positions

WHEN THE LEGS of both the male and the female are stretched straight out over each other, this is known as the clasping position. It is of two kinds, the side position and the supine position, according to the way in which the couple lie down. In the side position the male should invariably lie on his left side and cause the woman to lie on her right side, and this rule is to be observed in lying down with all kinds of women. When, after congress has begun in the clasping position, the woman presses her lover with her thighs, this is known as the pressing position. When the woman places one of her thighs across the thigh of her lover, it is known as the twining position. When a woman forcibly holds the lingam in her yoni after it is in, this is known as the mare's position. It is accomplished by practice only, and is chiefly found among the women of the Andhra country.

Rising, Pressing and Other Positions

WHEN THE FEMALE raises both of her thighs straight up, this is known as the rising position. When she raises both of her legs and places them on her lover's shoulders, this is known as the yawning position. When the legs are contracted, and so held by the lover before his bosom, this is known as the pressed position. When only one of the woman's legs is stretched out, this is known as the half-pressed position. When she places one of her legs on her lover's shoulder and stretches the other one out, and then places that leg on his shoulder while stretching out the other leg, continuing to alternate in similar fashion, this is known as the splitting of a bamboo. When one of the woman's legs is placed on the man's head and the other is stretched out, this is known as the fixing of a nail. It is learned by practice only.

The Crab, the Lotus and Other Positions

WHEN BOTH of the woman's legs are drawn up and placed on her stomach, this is known as the crab's position. When the thighs are raised and placed one upon the other, this is known as the packed position. When the shanks are placed one upon the other, this is known as the lotus-like position. And when a man, during congress, turns round and enjoys the woman without leaving her, while she embraces him round the back all the time, this is known as the turning position; it is to be learned only by practice.

Supported and Suspended Congress

WHEN A MAN and a woman support themselves on each other's bodies, or against a wall or pillar, and thus while standing engage in congress, this is known as the supported congress. When a man supports himself against a wall, and the woman, sitting on his hands joined together and held underneath her, throws her arms round his neck and, putting her thighs around his waist, moves herself by her feet, which are touching the wall against which the man is leaning, this is known as the suspended congress.

Of Congress like Animals

WHEN A WOMAN stands on her hands and feet like a quadruped, and her lover mounts her like a bull, the act is known as the congress of a cow. At this time everything that is ordinarily done on the bosom should be done on the back. In the same way, a couple can carry on the congress of a dog, the congress of a goat, the congress of a deer, the forcible mounting of an ass, the congress of a cat, the jump of a tiger, the pressing of an elephant, the rubbing of a boar, and the mounting of a horse. And in all these cases the characteristics of these different animals should be manifested by acting like them.

Congress Between One and Many

WHEN A MAN enjoys two women at the same time, both of whom love him equally, this is known as the united congress. When a man enjoys many women all together, it is called the congress of a herd of cows. In Gramaneri many young men enjoy a woman that may be married to one of them, either one after the other or all at the same time. Thus one of them holds her, another enjoys her, a third uses her mouth, a fourth holds her middle part, and in this way they go on enjoying her several parts in turn. The same things can be done when several men sit in company with one courtesan, or when one courtesan is alone with many men. Something of the same kind can be done by the women of the king's harem when they chance to get hold of a man.

Multiplying the Kinds of Congress

AN INGENIOUS person should be able to multiply the kinds of congress after the fashion of the different kinds of beasts and of birds. For these different kinds of congress, performed according to the usage of each country and the liking of each individual, generate love, friendship and respect in the hearts of women. One who is well acquainted with the science of love and knows his own strength, as also the tenderness, impetuosity and strength of the young woman, should act according to that knowledge. The various modes of enjoyment are not for all times or for all persons, but they should only be used at the proper time and in the proper places.

A Woman Acting the Part of a Man

WHEN A WOMAN sees that her lover is fatigued by constant congress, without having his desire satisfied, she should, with his permission, lay him down upon his back and come to his aid by acting his part. She may also do this to satisfy the curiosity of her lover, or her own desire for novelty. There are two ways of doing this. The first is when, during congress, she turns round and gets on top of her lover, in such a way as to continue the congress without interrupting the pleasure of it; and the other is when she acts the man's part from the beginning. At such a time, with flowers in her hair hanging loose, and her smiles broken by hard breathings, she should press upon her lover's bosom with her own breasts, and lowering her head frequently, should perform the same actions as he has done on other occasions, returning his blows and chaffing him.

The Work of a Man

WHATEVER IS DONE by a man to give pleasure to a woman is called the work of a man, and is as follows. While the woman is lying on his bed, and is (as it were) abstracted by his conversation, he should loosen the knot of her undergarments, and when she begins to dispute with him he should overwhelm her with kisses. Then, when his lingam is erect, he should touch her with his hands in various places, and gently manipulate various parts of her body. If the woman is bashful, and if it is the first time that they have come together, the man should place his hands between her thighs, which she will probably keep close together; and if she is a very young girl, he should first put his hands upon her breasts, which she will probably cover with her own hands, and under her armpits and on her neck. If, however, she is a seasoned woman, he should do whatever is agreeable either to him or to her, and whatever is fitting for the occasion.

On Satisfying a Woman

WHILE A MAN is doing to the woman what he likes best during congress, he should always make a point of pressing those parts of her body on which she turns her eyes. The signs of the enjoyment and satisfaction of the woman are as follows. Her body relaxes, she closes her eyes, she puts aside all bashfulness and shows an increasing willingness to unite the two organs as closely as possible. On the other hand, the signs of her want of enjoyment and satisfaction are as follows. She shakes her hands, she does not let the man get up, she feels dejected, bites the man, kicks him, and continues to go on moving after he has finished. In such cases the man should rub the yoni of the woman with his hand and fingers until it is softened, and after that is done he should proceed to put his lingam into her.

The Tongs, the Top and the Swing

WHEN A WOMAN acts the part of a man, these are among the acts she may perform. When the woman holds the lingam in her yoni, draws it in, presses it, and keeps it thus inside her for a long time, this practice is known as the pair of tongs. When, while engaged in congress, she turns round like a wheel, it is called the top. This is learned by practice only. On such an occasion the man may lift up the middle part of his body and the woman turn round her middle part, and then the position is known as the swing. When the woman is tired, she should place her forehead on that of her lover, and should by this means rest without disturbing the union of the organs; and when the woman has rested herself the man should turn round and begin the congress again.

Of the Auparishtaka or Mouth Congress

WHEN A MAN and a woman lie down in an inverted order, with the head of the one towards the feet of the other, and carry on mouth congress, this is called the congress of the crow. The people of eastern India do not resort to women who practise the Auparishtaka. The people of Ahichhatra resort to such women, but do nothing with them so far as the mouth is concerned. The people of Saketa do with these women every kind of mouth congress, while the people of Nagara do not practise it, but do every other thing. The people of the Shrasena country, on the southern bank of the Jumna, do everything without hesitation. Vatsyayana thinks that in all these things connected with love, everybody should act according to the custom of his own country and his own inclination.

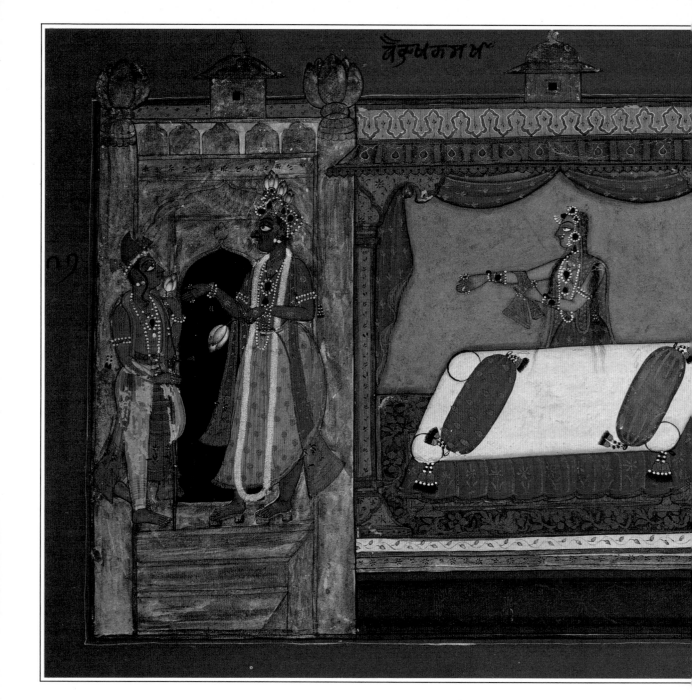

Where to Receive a Woman

IN THE PLEASURE ROOM, decorated with flowers and fragrant with perfumes, attended by his friends and servants, the man should receive the woman, who will come bathed and dressed, and will invite her to take refreshment and drink freely. He should then seat her on his left side and, holding her hair and also touching the end and knot of her garment, he should gently embrace her with his right arm. They should then carry on an amusing conversation on various subjects, and may also talk of things that would normally be considered risqué or unmentionable in society. They may sing and play on musical instruments, talk about the arts, and urge each other to drink. At last, when the woman is overcome with love and desire, the man should dismiss any companions he may have with him, giving them flowers, unguents and betel leaves; and then, when the two are left alone, they should act in the ways that have already been described.

At the End of the Congress

MODESTLY, and not looking at each other, the lovers should go separately to the washing-room. After this they should eat some betel leaves, and the man should with his own hand apply some pure sandalwood ointment to the body of the woman. He should then embrace her with his left arm, and with agreeable words cause her to drink from a cup held in his own hand. They can eat sweetmeats, and may drink fresh juice, soup, gruel, extracts of meat sherbet, the juice of mango fruits, the extract of the juice of the citron tree mixed with sugar, or anything known to be sweet, soft and pure. The lovers may also sit on the terrace of the palace or house, enjoy the moonlight and carry on an agreeable conversation. At this time, while the woman lies in his lap with her face towards the moon, her lover should show her the different planets, the morning star, the pole star, and the Great Bear. And so ends sexual congress.

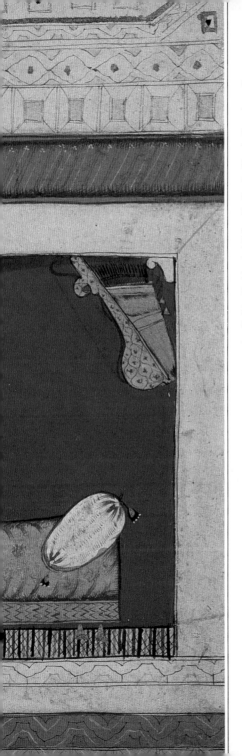

On Marriage

WHEN A GIRL of the same caste as her husband-to-be, and a virgin, is married in accordance with the precepts of the Scriptures, the results of such a union are the acquisition of Dharma and Artha, offspring, affinity, increase of friends, and untarnished love. For this reason a man should fix his affections upon a girl who is of good family, whose parents are alive, and who is three years or more younger than himself.

She should be born of a highly respectable family, possessed of wealth, well connected, and with many relations and friends. She should also be beautiful, of a good disposition, with lucky marks on her body, and with good hair, nails, teeth, ears, eyes and breasts, neither more nor less than they ought to be, and no one of them entirely wanting, and not troubled with a sickly body. Of course the man himself should also possess these qualities.

Gaining a Bride's Confidence

A MAN ACTING according to the inclinations of a girl should try to gain her over so that she will love him and place her confidence in him. A man does not succeed either by unquestioningly following the inclinations of a girl, or by wholly opposing them, and he should therefore adopt a middle course. Such a man knows how to make himself beloved by women, at the same time increasing their honour and creating confidence in them. But he who neglects a girl, thinking she is too bashful, is despised by her as a beast, ignorant of the workings of the female mind. Moreover, a girl forcibly enjoyed by one who does not understand the hearts of girls becomes nervous, uneasy and dejected, and suddenly begins to hate the man who has taken advantage of her; and then, since her love is not understood or returned, she sinks into despondency and becomes either a hater of mankind altogether, or, hating her own man, has recourse to other men.

How a Girl Shows Her Love

A GIRL ALWAYS shows her love by outward signs and actions. She never looks the man in the face, and becomes abashed when she is looked at by him; under some pretext she shows her limbs to him; she looks secretly at him, hangs down her head when she is asked some question by him, and answers in indistinct words and unfinished sentences; she delights to be in his company for a long time, speaks to her attendants in a peculiar tone to attract his attention when she is at a distance from him, and is reluctant to go from the place where he is; under some pretext or other she shows him different things, kisses and embraces a child sitting in her lap when he is present, shows kindness to his servants, avoids being seen by her lover when she is not dressed and ornamented, and always wears anything that he has given her.

How to Gain Over a Man

OLD AUTHORS say that although a girl loves the man ever so much, she should not offer herself, or make the first overtures, for a girl who does this loses her dignity and is liable to be scorned and rejected. Instead, when the man shows his wish to enjoy her, she should respond graciously but without changing her demeanour, as if unaware of his state of mind. But when he tries to kiss her she should resist him; when he begs to be allowed to have sexual intercourse with her she should let him only touch her private parts, making considerable difficulties; and though importuned by him, she should resist his attempts to have her. It is only when she is certain that she is truly loved, and that her lover is indeed devoted to her and will not change his mind, that she should give herself to him, and persuade him to marry her quickly. After losing her virginity she should tell her confidential friends about it.

Of a Man with Many Wives

A MAN MARRYING many wives should act fairly towards them all. He should not disregard or pass over their faults, but he should also not reveal to one wife the love, passion, bodily blemishes or confidences of another. No opportunity should be given to any one of them to speak to him about her rivals, and if one of them should begin to speak ill of another, he should chide her and tell her that she has exactly the same faults in her own character. He should please one of them by secret confidences, another by secret respect, and another by secret flattery, and he should please them all by going to gardens, by amusements, by presents, by honouring their relations, by telling them secrets, and lastly by loving unions. A young woman who is of a good temper, and who conducts herself according to the precepts of the Scriptures, wins her husband's attachment, and gains a superiority over her rivals.

Of the Love of Women and Men

IN LOVE the following circumstances are peculiar to the woman. She loves without regard to right or wrong, and does not try to gain over a man simply for the attainment of some particular purpose. Moreover, when a man first makes up to her she naturally shrinks from him, even though she may be willing to unite herself with him. But when his attempts to gain her over are renewed and repeated, she at last consents. Whereas a man, even though he has begun to love, may conquer his feelings from a regard for morality and wisdom. Or sometimes he makes an attempt to win the object of his affections and, having failed, leaves her alone for the future. Contrariwise, when a woman is once gained he often becomes indifferent to her. But as for the saying that a man does not care for what is easily gained, and only desires a thing which cannot be gained without difficulty, it is just idle talk.

Men Who Succeed with Women

THESE ARE AS FOLLOWS. Men well versed in the science of love. Men skilled in telling stories. Men acquainted with women from their childhood. Men who have secured their confidence. Men who send presents to them. Men who talk well. Men who do things that they like. Men who have not loved other women before. Men who act as messengers. Men who know their weak points. Men who are desired by good women. Men with close female friends. Men who are good looking. Men who have been brought up with women. Men who are their neighbours. Men who are devoted to sexual pleasures, even though these are enjoyed with their own servants. The lovers of the daughters of a girl's nurse. Men who have been lately married. Men who like picnics and pleasure parties. Men who are liberal. Men who are celebrated for being very strong (Bull men). Enterprising and brave men. Men who surpass women's husbands in learning and good looks, in good qualities, and in liberality. Men whose dress and manner of living are magnificent.

Seducing a Woman

WHEN A MAN is endeavouring to seduce one woman, he should not attempt to seduce any other at the same time. But after he has succeeded with the first, and enjoyed her for a considerable time, he can keep her affections by giving her presents that she likes, and then begin making up to another woman. When a man sees the husband of a woman going to some place not far from his house, he should not enjoy the woman then, even though she may be easily gained over at that moment. A wise man who is careful of his reputation should not think of seducing a woman who is apprehensive, timid, not to be trusted, well guarded, or possessed of a father-in-law or mother-in-law.

Of Waning Love

A WOMAN CAN always divine the state of mind, feelings and disposition of her lover from changes in his temper, manner and complexion. The behaviour of a waning lover may be described as follows. He gives the woman either less than is wanted, or something other than that which was asked for. He keeps her in hopes, but only by promises. He pretends to do one thing, and does something else. He does not fulfil her desires. He forgets his promises, or does something other than that which he has promised. He speaks with his own servants in a mysterious fashion. He sleeps in some other house under the pretext of having to do something for a friend. Finally, he speaks in private with the attendants of a woman with whom he was formerly acquainted.

On Personal Adornment

GOOD LOOKS, good qualities, youth and liberality are the chief and most natural means of making a person agreeable in the eyes of others. But in the absence of these a man or a woman must have resort to art. If a fine powder is made of various plants and applied to the wick of a lamp, which is made to burn with oil of blue vitriol, the black pigment it produces, when applied to the eyelashes, makes a person look lovely. The oil of the hogweed and other plants, if applied to the body, have the same effect. By eating the powder of the nelumbrium speciosum, the blue lotus and the mesna roxburghii with ghee and honey, a man becomes attractive in the eyes of others. And if the bone of a peacock or hyena is covered with gold and tied on the right hand, it produces the same result.

Recipes for Sexual Vigour

THE MEANS OF PRODUCING love and sexual vigour should be learned from the science of medicine, from the Vedas, from those who are adepts in the arts of magic, and from confidential relatives. No means should be tried which are doubtful in their effects, which are likely to cause injury to the body, which involve the death of animals, or which bring us into contact with impure things. Such means should only be used as are holy, acknowledged to be good, and approved of by Brahmans and friends. Among these means are the following. A man obtains sexual vigour by drinking milk mixed with sugar, the root of the uchchata plant, the piper chaba, and liquorice. Drinking milk, mixed with sugar and having the testicle of a ram or goat boiled in it, is also productive of vigour. And if a man mixes rice with sparrow eggs, and having boiled this in milk, adds to it ghee and honey, and drinks much of it, he will be able to enjoy innumerable women.

Congress with an Elephant Woman

IF A MAN IS unable to satisfy a Hastini, or Elephant woman, he should have recourse to various means to excite her passion. At the beginning he should rub her yoni with his hand or fingers, and not begin to have intercourse with her until she becomes excited or experiences pleasure. This is one way of exciting a woman. Or he may make use of certain Apadravyas, or things which are put on or around the lingam to supplement its length or its thickness, so as to fit it to the yoni. In the opinion of Babhravya these Apadravyas should be made of gold, silver, copper, iron, ivory, buffalo's horn, various kinds of wood, tin or lead, and should be soft, cool, provocative of sexual vigour, and well fitted to serve the intended purpose.

Vatsyayana, however, says that they may be made according to the natural liking of each individual.

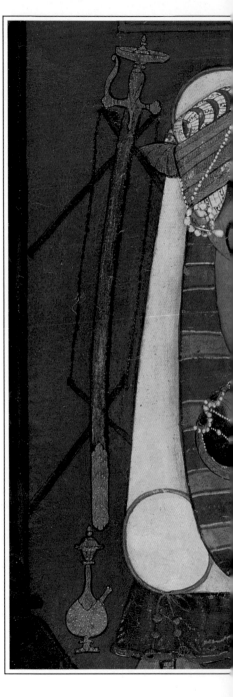

On the *Kama Sutra* and Vatsyayana

THE *Kama Sutra* was composed, according to the precepts of the Scriptures and for the benefit of the world, by Vatsyayana while he was leading the life of a religious student and wholly engaged in the contemplation of the Divine. This work is not intended to be used merely as an instrument for satifying our desires. A person acquainted with the true principles of this science, and who preserves his Dharma, Artha and Kama (religious merit, wealth and love) and has regard for established custom, is sure to obtain mastery over his senses. In short, an intelligent and prudent person, attending to Dharma and Artha, and attending to Kama also, without becoming the slave of his passions, obtains success in everything he may undertake.

ACKNOWLEDGEMENTS

The Publisher would like to thank the following for their kind permission to reproduce the paintings in this book:

Bridgeman Art Library, London/British Library, London 68; **/Fitzwilliam Museum, University of Cambridge** 12; **/National Museum of India, New Delhi** 62, 66-67; **/Private Collection** 30-31, 56, 70-71, 74; **/Victor Lownes Collection, London** 10-11, 14, 22, 23, 24-25, 26, 27, 32, 33, 34-35, 36, 37, 38-39, 40, 42-43, 41, 44, 45, 46-47,48-49, 50, 51, 52-53, 57, 58, 60, 72, 75, 76-77, 78; **/Victoria and Albert Museum** cover, 13, 15, 16-17, 18, 20-21, 28-29, 54-55, 61, 64-65, 69, 73.